D0934350

At Home With Nature

At Home With Nature

Great Interiors From The Great Outdoors

by Susan Fredman

Published by
The
Ashley
Group

Copyright© 2000 by
Susan Fredman & Associates, Ltd.
425 Huehl Rd., Unit 6B
Northbrook, Illinois 60062
847.509.4121 FAX 847.509.4111
www.susanfredman.com

All rights reserved. No part of this book may be reproduced in any form without written permission of the copyright owners. All images in this book have been reproduced with the knowledge and prior consent of the artists concerned, and no responsibility is accepted by producer, publisher or printer for any infringement of copyright or otherwise arising from the contents of this publication. Every effort has been made to ensure that credits accurately comply with information supplied.

Published by
The Ashley Group
A Cahners® Business Information Company
1350 Touhy Ave.
Des Plaines, Illinois 60018
847.390.2882   FAX 847.390.2902
www.ashleygroup@cahners.com

Concept & Design: Paul A. Casper
Editor-in-Chief: Dana Felmly
Editor: LaDonna Willems
Art Direction: Bill Patton, Kim Foundos, Maura Gonsalves
Group Production Director: Steve Perlstein

Photographers
Janet Mesic Mackie, Chicago, IL: James Yochum, Sawyer, MI: Jill Buckner Wingfield, Roswell, GA:
Linda Oyama Bryan, Wilmette, IL, Cover, p. 2, 16, 17, 18, 19, 20, 22, 23, 36, 48, 49, 50, 60, 84, 98, 99, 100
Brian Fritz, Northbrook, IL: Jon Miller, Chicago, IL: Charles Gurche, Spokane, WA: Ray Hillstrom, Chicago, IL:
Paul Rezendes, Royalston, MA: Jim Steinberg, Steamboat Springs, CO:
Dianne Dietrich Leis, Dietrich Stock Photo: Dick Dutuch, Dietrich Photography

Printed in China

ISBN 1-5886204-3-3

First Edition

For Terri, who provides the context for me to live my
dreams. And to Amanda and Jessica, I am so grateful for
the gift of children and what loving you provide us all.

Contents

Introduction

This book is the documentation of an interior design practice that spans 25 years. We at Susan Fredman & Associates Ltd. celebrated our 25th Anniversary during the year 2000. Like most milestones, this year gave us the opportunity to look back at the years behind us and see how far we've come.

In gathering together all of the thoughts and the photography for this book, we have spent a great deal of time wondering, investigating, and dissecting what might be the common thread that winds its way through all of these 25 years of work. My work is transitional for those who ask; very traditional upon request; and of course, some of our clients lean toward the very contemporary taste. So there is no single "type" of style that defines my body of work.

Making Your Space Your Own

How have I been able to "switch" styles and palettes at will? What happens between a designer and a client to accomplish these results? What special magic is worked when a relationship clicks? These are the questions that define what we do at Susan Fredman & Associates. This process that we work so hard to achieve can work miracles to give your home a unique feeling that is precisely your own.

No two homes are the same—they shouldn't be! And we bring to you the essence of that individual element. We provide that indescribable, almost indistinguishable commodity that gives interior spaces the qualities that are specific to you—the little touches that make you feel nourished and help you not just to live, but to thrive in your environment. That contrast of texture, the combination of natural and man-made… these are the things that give us a space of peacefulness. Our very own sanctuary from the chaos of the world outside.

This is why interior design is so important.

For the Love of Nature

As I ponder my particular style as it has evolved over the last 25 years, these are the thoughts that spring to mind. And I think I have found that common thread. No matter what shape my work takes, no matter what style my clients' request, I see throughout all of my work the simple love of nature and natural materials. It is the contrast that natural materials provide when combined with other materials that makes things sing. Nature is everywhere. It surrounds us at every moment. And most designers use natural materials as much as they possibly can. We give conscious thought to the combination of these textures and to the way that people feel in the environments we create. I have devoted my career to making people's interior spaces the kind of places that really nurture them.

I have spent my life trying to understand how people think and how they live. It is particularly important for me to understand what my clients' hopes and dreams are. And it has been my life's work to provide my clients with the settings that nurture their souls. This is, admittedly, an ambitious dream and an unusual burden, but it is a dream that has lived up to the challenge for the past 25 years, and it continues to hold my attention to this day.

> *"Homesteading, as I envision it, is our process of redefining the purpose of the home to fit a new set of lifestyle values. I think of homesteading today as an attitude of mind that recognizes that there are few natural places remaining in the world for pioneers to settle."*
> ■ *Louis Sagar*

Getting to Know You

In the process of designing an interior for a client, we get to know each other very well. I want my clients to stretch and grow in the process, so I bring them things they would not have thought of, had access to, or imagined for themselves. I've even had clients tentatively say, "These colors don't really match, do they? I mean, green and brown don't go together." And I answer, "Well, look at the trees and leaves. They match!"

The trust is built one step at a time. I trust their dream, and they trust my instincts. And we both grow in the process, and beautiful, livable rooms are the end result. Step inside these pages with me, and I will show you what my life's work has been about. And maybe you, too, will come to see that green and brown really do go together!

It has been an honor to work with the people whose homes grace these pages. I have utmost respect for them for entrusting me with the care of a place as precious as their own homes.

Enjoy the journey!

Susan Fredman

■ *The glorious color of fall foliage, the intricate textures of bark and wood, the delicate veins in a leaf...trees and leaves are nature's gifts to us. In this entertainment area, the warm color and texture of wood are gifts for the soul as they create a cozy backdrop for unique southwestern accessories and wrought iron furnishings.*

Into the Woods

You can find so much in the arms of a tree. Shade. Shelter. Sanctuary. Trees are palaces for squirrels and condominiums for nesting birds. They are jungle gyms for the adventurous neighborhood kids. They are inspiration for artists and, for the average cat, trees are the perfect hideout from stalking dogs.

When paired with a combination of aged and new brick, the intricate texture and grain in wood forms a perfect marriage. This Gre Room expresses the beauty of wood by combining different types in the same pie in order to celebrate the difference in character and grain—there's even a rougl hewn "stump" complete with a knot natural hole.

14

Nature's Finest

We see them everyday, without even looking. Perhaps that's why we so often take the beauty of trees for granted. You have to stop yourself and look closely, consciously, to notice the amazing way that green blends with brown. (And you thought green and brown didn't match!)

They go all out in the fall, just before their winter hibernation. Showering us with a palette of the most robust yellows and flaming oranges. Here in the Midwest, if you go on a drive through the country at just the right time in October, you are guaranteed to have to pull off the road, turn off the engine, and stare. Because there is nothing like a forested hill dressed in its best fall colors. It defies adequate description.

"A woodland in full color is awesome as a forest fire, in magnitude at least, but a single tree is like a dancing tongue of flame to warm the heart."

■ *Hal Borland*

And the best thing about trees is that their splendor is not limited to their foliage. They are beautiful right down to the core. You've seen the rings of years within a tree's trunk, the circular pattern that holds so many seasons of stories. The bark is beautiful, too, with its many brown ridges and teardrops of golden sap.

That Forest Feeling

Trees are soothing to us on a cellular level. You may not even realize it with your mind, but your body does. Take a walk through your local forest preserve and feel the way your whole body relaxes. You start breathing deeper, walking slower, smiling to yourself.

If we let them, trees will comfort us and heal us in places we didn't even realize we were aching. They lift so many arms to the sky, bury so many roots in the soil, welcome so many creatures to their branches. They are mothers and fathers, caretakers and guardians to all.

And, when you bring a tree into your home, you bring in that forest feeling. The warm solidity of the wood itself, the deep greens and reds and browns of its outer shell. A tree will change your entire environment. It will welcome you home.

Putting Down Roots

To create an environment that embodies the same spirit of the woodland, you have to have a good understanding of people's relationship with trees.

■ *When we think of trees at night, we imagine little woodland creatures sleeping inside, safe and secure. A bedroom enhanced with natural wood can create that same feeling of protection. These three bedrooms utilize fall and spring colors to further evoke the sense of security.*

As wood evokes a feeling of security, stone offers a sense of permanence. Together in one room, they relax us as they make us feel that all is well and we are protected and safe. Here the colors of earth, autumn foliage and birch bark join with wood and stone to make this room feel even more like a safe haven from the winds outside.

Many of the things we love about trees are directly connected to the way they make us feel. We watch them sink their roots deep into the earth, and we feel grounded. Think of the way you feel when you are surrounded by the massive trunks of trees that have stood their ground since before your grandfather was born. There is something very stable and comforting about that image.

Perhaps that's why so many of us fight so hard to save trees and forests. Without them, we would feel unsteady.

Trees are amazing combinations of opposites. They are towers of strength—every year they face the storms of winter only to burst forth with new buds each spring. Yet trees are also graceful—the way they bend in the wind can be as beautiful as a ballet. As pedestals for these tables, these beautifully gnarled stumps exhibit their strength, and when topped with the shining liquidity of glass, the result is magical. When the graceful lines of a tree are emulated in a beautiful hanging lamp, the grace of the tree is made manifest.

"One touch of nature makes the whole world kin."

■ *Shakespeare*

Many of the homes that I have designed with a prominent wood theme are people's second homes-their vacation or weekend homes, most of which are located out in the country. These clients feel a deeply rooted connection to the earth and to the trees themselves, so when I bring trees into the decor of their home, they are delighted. It makes them feel like they are outside, in the midst of nature, all the time.

■ *Even in a new kitchen, the visual strength and natural beauty of wood can create a sense of history. The country cabinetry, butcher-block countertop, wide planked floors and antique accessories combine to create an up-to-date kitchen that evokes a feeling of years gone by.*

When you are surrounded by natural wood, you tend to feel more casual, more loose and at ease. It's a picnic-in-the park kind of feeling. You know you don't have to be proper and formal-you can relax, be yourself, breathe out. Having wood in our homes inspires us to become more playful, more rested, more mellow and content.

It's the same way we would feel if we were outside, in the woods, sheltered beneath the arches of leaves. Not a care in the world. Who could ask for more?

■ *Through the use of wood, this kitchen breakfast area conveys a sense of strength and permanence that can restore the soul. This feeling is intensified by the use of granite for the tabletop. The natural color of wood in the rough-hewn, shaped stools, the wide planked floor and the ceiling and walls lends a golden glow to the room.*

"Us sing and dance, make faces and give flower bouquets, trying to be loved. You ever notice that trees do everything to git attention we do, except walk?"

■ *Alice Walker, in The Color Purple*

■ *Green grassy fields have a soothing quality that make one want to sink into a peaceful slumber. Who can forget the feeling of lying in a green field and looking at the sky on a clear summer day? Bringing the color of moss indoors is like bringing the outdoors inside. In this bedroom, the moss green walls create a pleasant contrast to the white ceiling bedspread.*

It *Is* Easy Being Green

There is nothing in the world like the smell of newly mown grass. It speaks of summer and sunshine, and all the secret hidden things that hide beneath its cover. In farmer's fields and city blocks, grass calls with the same quiet urging.

We want to strip off our shoes and socks and feel the cool blades beneath our feet. We want to stretch out full-length on its mossy carpet and rest for awhile. We want to regress to age nine and run through the clover, shrieking with delight.

The Greener Side

Grass offers a green promise of relaxation. It has so many textures, so many moods-from the spiky green stalks of beach grasses sprouting from sandy dunes to the velvety sponge of moss on the shady side of a woodland tree.

So much of what we love about grass lies in its color. Many of us spend a good amount of cash trying to get our lawns that perfectly smooth shade of green, without any hint of an errant dandelion patch. But, just as with texture, there are so many options of green.

Perhaps that's one of the reasons we love to bring green inside-it gives us so much to play with. And, in a very literal sense, green brings the outdoors in. It provides a grounding, soothing balance to our inner world. In every shade and texture, it reminds us of its vibrant twin that lives outside beneath the sunshine.

A Green for All Seasons

There seems to be a green for every mood. The bright spring green of vitality and the muted moss green that promises safe harbor. The light and playful tones of neon green and the soothing sight of seafoam. The natural khaki color that disappears into the background and the iridescence of bottle green.

In designing a room, it is often the color that brings balance. It is our job, as the designers of an interior space, to look at a room and decide how it flows and what it will function as. And then we decide what we want to look at. Color often helps us create this focal point. With it, we can create a background and a foreground, symmetry and asymmetry. Sometimes color can be used to strengthen a room, and sometimes it provides all of the friction.

"To cherish what remains of the Earth and to foster its renewal is our only legitimate hope of survival."

■ *Wendell Berry*

This room makes one think of green meadows and fields, alive with flowers. From the pale green of the walls to the green and white leaf-patterned quilt, the final effect is restful and contemplative. Who wouldn't want to sink into a deep restful slumber in a room like this, or read a book by the fireplace?

29

■ *Grasses woven together, wrapping, twisting, bending, bonding to gain strength and give comfort and even hope. In this room, that strength is felt from the sturdy woven rug stretched across the floor and from the wicker coffee table that awaits teacups, saucers, dishes and whatever else comes its way.*

These are decisions that must be made consciously, deliberately, with intention and foresight. In one of the rooms in my own house, it is the soft sage green paint on the walls that holds the whole room together. This was a specific choice I made, to create a room that could serve many functions and still feel unified. The green of the walls makes the environment in that room soft, relaxed and whole.

A Calming Influence

Sometimes color doesn't need to be the glue-it can just fade and disappear and provide a subtle, reassuring mood. But, as subtle as it may appear, this mood doesn't happen by chance.
Usually, with no planning, a room tends toward chaos rather than calm.

For example, think of the doctors' offices you've visited throughout your life. The waiting rooms there are famous for having been created with no thought at all. There are a bunch of chairs, scattered magazines, maybe a few miscellaneous art prints. This is a room to sit and wait in, so often it doesn't get a lot of forethought up front.

But think about how those rooms make you feel. Rooms with no background or foreground. No specific place for your eyes to rest. No planning of mood and balance. It's all just... there. And that's why you feel uncomfortable. Just a few minutes in a room like that, and you begin to squirm. You don't belong-nothing belongs. And your mind and your body react to that.

■ *Touches of green can be like points of light in a room. Green grass holds the promise c summer, and all of the things that go along with summer: sunshine, relaxation and endles days of everlasting freedom.*

Now imagine if you were in a waiting room swathed in a gentle mossy color. Surrounded by the texture and tones of a woodland meadow. In a setting like that, you might even be able to forget that you came to have your teeth drilled.

Nature has much to teach us about color. Next time you find yourself in a grassy patch, take a moment or two to observe the blending of greens, the texture of the plants that bend beneath your feet. The simple way the green of the leaves and the brown of the tree bark balance each other so beautifully.

And then take that feeling home with you and make it uniquely your own.

Playing with Fire

Have you ever lost yourself to the spell of a flame?
First you notice the cobalt blue at its base, a blue which fades to purple and then to a determined red,
flaring up into the brightest white at its tip. It dances and bows like an uncontrollable ballerina,
dipping down to answer the unseen breath of wind and then suddenly flaring upright again.

A fiery sunset paints the landscape in dramatic tones of purple, yellow and orange—we can take the drama and beauty we find in our natural world and use it for inspiration in our interior spaces. These throw pillows give off a fiery glow with their red and yellow tones contrasted by the blue colors in the quilt. Using this color scheme in a room immediately sets a mood of warmth and brilliance and reminds one of fire's mystique.

You can lose yourself in a candle flame, a fireplace, a bonfire. Each holds the same magic at its center-a force that we cannot understand, so we are irrevocably drawn in, fascinated.

"Nature is man's teacher. She unfolds her treasures to his search, unseals his eye, illumes his mind, and purifies his heart; an influence breathes from all the sights and sounds of her existence."

■ *Alfred Billings Street*

Ring of Fire

Fire, at its most basic vanilla scented-candle or family campfire level, comforts us. At its most powerful, it is an awe-inspiring force of nature.

It is a fierce predator, devouring whole forests and acres of land in just a few hours. It blazes, and we do our best to control it, but it has a magnificent power of its own. In the end we usually win-the fire dies out. But what an awesome trail of blackened ashes it leaves in its wake. It's part of the endless cycle of natural life. The fire dies, the rains come, new forests grow and the circle begins again.

On a much smaller scale, fire can be warm and friendly. It adorns our homes with tiny tongues of candle-flame. It roasts our marshmallows and toasts our hot dogs. It makes us feel warm and lazy as we doze in front of a fireplace after a day of building snowmen. It speaks to us with crackles and sparks and makes us feel at home. But deep within those bluish flames, the same power that sparks the raging forest fire is always present.

■ *The element of fire colors this library and makes it into the perfect spot to curl up with a book. From the reddish glow of the natural wood to the rust and purple in the upholstery, this room is a warm haven.*

House Afire

Perhaps that is why decorating with fire is not for the faint of heart. Because fire, when used in interior design, is always about the color red. And you can't be bashful when you use red in a room.

You have to be willing to play when you use red. And you have to be comfortable with it. After all, a home is a place to feel a connection with other human beings, even if you live alone. Keep that thought at the back of your mind when you begin to design your personal space. The decor should never overpower the sense of humanity.

There are some spaces where you know that human beings come in second. The massive rotunda of the Field Museum in Chicago. Every inch of the Louvre in Paris. Places like these were designed to keep you focused on the art and the artifacts, and keep your mind off of yourself. They are overwhelming, overpowering spaces, and they have every right to be. But these are not the kind of spaces that you live in.

■ *The peaceful serenity of this room comes from the browns, reds and golds that create a welcoming aura that is hard to resist. It's a clear demonstration of how color can truly transform your world.*

■ *In past centuries, man has turned to fire for comfort, and the modern pilgrim continues to find solace in it. The warm brown and red tones found in this sun porch are evocative of the warmth found in the colors of a flickering fire on a cold night. Through design, we truly can create a world for ourselves that is unique if we follow nature's lead.*

Keeping It Human

As an interior designer, my job is to never forget that the purpose of a home is to nurture the people who live there. So how do you use fire in a nurturing manner? Is it even possible? Think of a glowing sunset-the burnished oranges and fiery reds. It is impressive. It is vibrant. And yet it still has the capability to nurture us. That's the type of fire you can use in a living space.

> *"Love is a fire. But whether it is going to warm your hearth or burn down your house, you can never tell."*
>
> ■ *Joan Crawford*

One of my clients came to me with a picture torn from a magazine. The main feature of the room in the magazine was a bright orange wall. My client pointed to this wall and said, "I want to feel like this."

And so we created a strong and fiery room that you can still plop down in and make yourself at home. The trick is to harness the intensity of the fire image, to mold that energy into an aura of strength. You have to provide balance and power, all within a small manageable space, so you don't disturb what I like to call "the human scale."

The use of skylights and translucent windows in this powder room create a sense of lightness and openness. The liberal use of wood and colors on the doors under the sink ground this room, yet the delightful, hand-painted icons remind us of the magic that is the essence of the world above us.

And when it works, it is magnificent. As dazzling as the most phenomenal sunset, and as comfortable as a backyard campfire. It is dynamic decor with a distinctively human voice.

It is fire with personality.

The sky offers us so much—a feeling of freedom, a lightness of being, a sense that the world is limitless and ours alone. Through the use of light colors in the sofa, the curve of the wood detailing at the bottom of the open-railed staircase and the airiness of the table legs, this Great Room evokes the joyous feeling of openness and peace that is the essence of sky. Yet, lest we go flying off into the blue, this room also grounds us through the use of earth and fire hues in the rug and cushions.

Into the
Wild Blue Yonder

It is the essence of imagination. The stuff of dreams, the inspiration of ten thousand flights of fancy. It is always above us and yet somehow surrounding us, too. It is our magical, mystical, endless field of blue. The sky.

46

■ *Sky comes in many colors, just look outside. The silvery ceiling in this contemporary room evokes the feeling of the sky on a late November day. The view through the upper glass panel and into the adjoining room looks beyond the horizon into the future.*

There's something about the sky that awakens a bird in all of us. We feel the urge to fly. The sky promises freedom and release. And it is forever blue. Even on the cloudiest day, a hint of blue sneaks through. And at night, studded with patterns of stars, the blue darkens, but it's still there.

In the dusty blue of twilight, the periwinkle of sunrise, the azure tones of a summer day and the cold crisp aquamarine of a winter afternoon, our skies are always blue.

Dreaming in Blue

It's a color that holds you. It captures your attention, makes you draw a quick breath as you step outside and remark, "Wow. Sky sure is blue today." It entices you to sprawl on your back on a knobby hillside and stare into its depths to count airplanes or find Mickey Mouse in the clouds.

And more than anything, our blue sky gives us the ability to step outside ourselves and dream. Somehow, just looking at the sky, you know you can do the nearly impossible.

How amazing, then, to transport that feeling into the place you call home. To put the power of dreams, the infinite freedom of the sky, into your living room, your bedroom. To keep it as a constant reminder of how you feel when you walk outside, look up, and melt into the blue.

"We had the sky up there, and we used to lay on our backs and look up at them, and discuss whether they was made or just happened."

■ *Mark Twain*

Infinite Possibilities

Nothing says "sky" in a room like the color blue. It's a color that suggests infinite possibilities. In any shade, any mixture of tones, the color blue creates a foreground, a place for the eyes to focus. A startling stroke of blue here and there-a pillow, a chair, a wall-makes a bold statement and yet makes you feel at home.

■ *In this bathroom, a sense of sky is everywhere. Here, windows and skylights let in the light, birds perch atop airy accessories, the unique scrimshaw sculpture points to the sky and the two mirrors reproduce these delightful images over and over.*

I have a client, an alumnus of the University of Michigan, who told me that she wanted to use her school colors of maize and blue to create an environment that she loved. She didn't know how to do it, she just knew that she wanted to feel some sort of connection to her past and her future with her children. And so her room became a blue sky room.

It's amazing what happens when you make a true connection with the people who entrust you with the responsibility of creating their personal spaces. They come to you, often with no concrete idea of how they want to feel or what they want to communicate. But then they let you into their lives a little, and you see exactly what needs to be done.

Above and Beyond

Earth meets sky, and the result is an open, inviting, comfortable living space. Plenty of external light streams through the windows to the right, adding to the spacious feeling.

With my University of Michigan client, the choice of the color blue was obvious. It is a color that looks out to the horizon and back to the past all at the same time. In this case, we wanted to use blue in a way that could be interpreted as both background and foreground, all at once.

So we added texture, color, and detail and worked with the architect until we had a room that held the same kind of nostalgia and hope that you can find in the sky on a clear afternoon. It managed to be both playful and serious, which is one of the best benefits of using blue. The color lets you be sophisticated without becoming self-important.

And the best part... now my client loves to be at home in her house.

Next time you find yourself staring up at the heavens, whether it's on a sunny summer afternoon or on a clear cold midnight, try to capture that feeling. Then go inside and splash some blue around your rooms. You just may find yourself dreaming more.

Sometimes it's good to get your feet off the ground.

The leopard skin motif on these adjoining chairs transforms the environment of this room from the simply ordinary to the existing. With a little inspiration from the natural world, we can create an interior world that never fails to surprise or amaze us.

52

The Birds and the Bees
(and the Bears)

Almost everyone has a favorite animal. A creature that makes us feel hopeful and lighthearted all at once. Because just looking at it, you know God must have a sense of humor.

Little girls dream of ponies. Boys want dogs. Some of us collect cats, while others favor ferrets. Some go to the zoo to stare at the dolphins while others want to see the polar bears. Some of us are left breathless at the sight of a deer bounding over a fence. Still others find their pulse racing when they hear a wolf howl. Whoever you are, whatever your mood, there's got to be an animal for you.

"All animals, except man, know that the principal business of life is to enjoy it... and they do enjoy it as much as man and other circumstances will allow."

■ *Samuel Butler*

Making Friends

It's amazing, really, what animals do to us. They become our friends, our allies. They are the helpless ones who allow us to rescue them. They inspire us with their wild freedom. And mostly, they make us laugh. Just the sight of a duck-billed platypus is enough to send anyone into gales of laughter. And there are simpler comedians-kittens chasing string across a hardwood floor. Squirrels trying to find that long lost acorn. A Basset Hound trying to walk through snow drifts. Wrinkly turtle necks. Warm puppy breath. Rambunctious baby goats.

Bringing the outside world inside reminds us that we are connected with the environment through nature and will always be. This room evokes a sense of grace and simplicity, while also reflecting the owner's personality with its telltale humorous touches. The bear at the doorway brings a sense of the wilderness into the room, and brilliant sunflowers provide a counterpoint to the dark shag rug.

The Wild West symbolizes freedom and individuality, and horses are emblematic of those ideals, as are these ornately crafted saddles. Cowboys have always respected the power and beauty of nature, and this room evokes these time-honored attitudes. The small touches in the room add a sense of completion, and also bring it into the modern world with a bold mixture of pastels and bright southwestern colors.

Only by embracing nature and claiming our place in the cycle of life can we truly free ourselves, and find the peace and serenity that we are all seeking. The decor of this room with its natural wood paneling and southwestern motif carried throughout is modern yet rustic. One is instantly transported to another world—a place where all creatures exist in harmony and tranquility.

A close-up of these throw pillows reveals animals galore in all shapes and sizes. From the stately king of the jungle, the lion, to the steadfast camel and the predatory tiger, these color-fully decorated pillows remind us that we are also of the natural world with all of its splendor and grace.

60

We've immortalized our animal friends in Disney cartoons. We've read Dr. Doolittle and fantasized about what they would say to us if only they could talk. We take a guess at which animal we'd most like to be. Because in so many ways, they remind us of ourselves. They have societies and hierarchies, mates and offspring. We've learned so many things about ourselves by watching the animals first.

> *"We are part of the earth and it is part of us. The perfumed flowers are our sisters; the deer, the horse, the great eagle; these are our brothers. All things are connected like the blood which unites one's family."*
>
> ■ *Chief Seattle*

Welcome to the Zoo

So it's no wonder we want to bring them into our homes. We welcome them inside with paintings and plaques, sculptures and figurines. We mount their likenesses on our walls to remind us of the things we love most about them. Some bring with them the breath of the outdoors, wild and rugged. Others just make us feel at home. In a room that features animals, you can't take yourself too seriously.

Sometimes it's not even about a specific favorite animal, it's just about the playful feeling that animals inspire and then how you translate that feeling into a space. I had a client who wanted a room that was comfortable—a room to "play" in. Although the client never said, "I'm really into cowboy stuff," that's how the room turned out. It's a cowboy room.

And yet, there are no horses or cows in the room; not even buffalo, for that matter. The lighthearted "cowboy" mood is, instead, created by suggestion. Rich textures. A bold use of color. And faux hide-covered chairs that simply suggest the presence of an animal. My client loves this room. For me, it was all about enticing and engaging them, asking them to stretch their ability to look and to understand color and texture.

I had one client who already had a great art collection of old French posters. There was no specific animal theme here, but in creating a room that could handle the art collection, the animal attitude came out. The room needed bold colors and fabrics that could complement the posters and yet not feel overpowering. The animal theme had the strength to handle all these colors and textures and larger sized objects without getting lost.

Room to Play

Sometimes it's a much more obvious theme-cast iron light fixtures in the shape of buffalo or a stuffed grizzly standing in the corner. It can be a subtle use of texture or the focal point of the room. But no matter how you produce that animal feeling, you'll know it's a success when you've got a room you just want to sit down in, put your feet up, and laugh.

This is why I love interior design, and why I think it's so important for all of us. The secret is establishing that trusting relationship with your client-hearing what they are really trying to express beneath the words. And when your relationship clicks, when you understand them and they know that you do, that's when a room comes together almost without thinking.

You just instinctively know what needs to happen so that you can help your client feel the way they want to feel in their rooms. In this case, the end result was a room that brings a smile to your face. A room that says "breathe out." A room that invites you to relax as soon as you cross the threshold.

That is the magic of the animal theme.

The natural world is a source of inspiration for this room. The warmth and vitality of the southwest is evoked with the brightly colored flooring, while the wood paneling is contrasted by figures of bison that almost appear to be walking across the great plains. The painting of the cowboy on the wall is playful and almost whimsical, but the room still retains a sense of elegance and charm.

Rocks, stones and minerals root us in both the past and the present, because they are timeless and everlasting. They can also create elegance as this beautifully appointed powder room illustrates. From the glimmering gold that frames the mirror to the antique, marble topped vanity, this room elicits a feeling of quiet elegance and restrained splendor.

Stones, Rocks and Minerals Oh My

They have outlasted more than we could ever hope to see in a dozen lifetimes. Forming the foundation of much of our environment, the rocks and stones that surround us seem to say that they always have been, and they always will be.

Even when the earth shakes, they are permanent fixtures. In spite of all this blue ball of earth has seen, the mountains remain. They are a testament to an eternity we cannot fathom. On their grandest scale, they are large enough to take our breath away. And in pebble form, they fascinate us still. It's as if we can still feel the slice of mountain from which these stones were born.

The stones used to build the central wall of this living spac help to create a visual effect that is almost a merging of th interior and exterior spaces in our world. The wood paneled skylight ceiling brings in natural outdoor light all year round, and even the lampshade has a texture that is reminiscent of stone.

66

Since the beginning of time, we have borrowed from them to build our homes, our cities, our fortresses and our roadways. They offer us strength, stability and security. And they intrigue us with their variegated textures and cool depths.

"Those who contemplate the beauty of the earth find reserves of strength that will endure as long as life lasts."

■ *Rachel Carson*

They like to catch you off guard, too. The smaller minerals and gems hide inside nondescript rocks, waiting for the right ray of sunlight before they show off their true colors and startle you with their beauty.

Nothin' but a Rock Hound

Rocks and stones, minerals and gems have for ages been one of mankind's biggest obsessions. How many lifelong rockhounds began their career with an innocent piece of beach glass that they found on the beach and then realized that they couldn't stop looking, scanning, searching for the next amazing find.

There is a beauty inherent in gems and rocks of all kinds that makes us want to collect them. And not only because they are beautiful, but also because of the way they fascinate us with their shapes and intricate interweaving of mineral deposits. Did you ever pick up a stone and think, "This rock looks like my State!" or "Wow! This stone is shaped like an arrowhead!" Perhaps you've gazed at larger rocks like Man of the Mountain in New Hampshire, now immortalized on quarters, and seen the unmistakable image of an eye, a large nose, or a jutting chin. Seeing personal things, or even ourselves, in these physical objects gives us a connection to them.

We're so accustomed to having minerals and stones as a daily part of our lives that we wouldn't know what to do without their constant presence. The silvery strength of iron, the impassive solidity of granite. The glit-

■ *In this bathroom, the warm
brown textures and tones of
the tiles and countertop are
offset by the shine of glass
and metal.*

ter of a vein of gold buried in the wall of a mountain. The crystals that gleam from the center of a geode accidentally split open. The surprising beauty of polished tin, reflecting your own image back at you.

Just the Right Touch

It is not a novel concept, then, to bring these gems, minerals, stones and rocks into our homes. We've been doing it, in one way or another, for thousands and thousands of years.

But we have other materials to choose from for stability in our structures now, which means we can be more selective about our rocks. We can use them as decorative elements. We can make them the centerpiece of a room now instead of just the foundation. Now we can build stone fireplaces just because we love the rugged look of it. We can use stone to tile our walls and floors. And hunks of rock can now serve as tables and chairs.

> *"Climb the mountains and get their good tidings. Nature's peace will flow into you as sunshine flows into trees. The winds will blow their freshness into you, and the storms their energy, while cares will drop off like falling leaves."*
>
> ■ *John Muir*

Gems and minerals, once inside, can astonish you with their power to complete a room. A little tin here and a bit of granite countertop there, and you'll be amazed at how much these elemental pieces add to your environment. They accent the dark corners with tiny pinpoints of light. They transform a simple countertop into a masterpiece of polished beauty. They turn a tile floor into an amazing display of textures and tones.

At the most elemental level, gems and minerals, rocks and stones add just the right touch of contrast to our environment. Combine the gloss of metal with the soft look of oak, and you have a masterpiece of pleasant contradiction. The truth is, we need friction like this to keep us happy.

■ *Natural stone is used for the tiles on this kitchen wall, and the metallic finish of the cabinet's face picks up the sheen of the center island with its finished stone countertop. Polished clay pots continue the stone motif, which is carried throughout the design of this kitchen.*

The Attraction of Opposites

Most of the time we don't realize that we're doing it-always looking for friction, disparity, contrast. In the crafting and creation of harmonious interiors, it is this polarity of objects, textures, colors and materials that make a room really sing.

The beauty of contrast is that it works in any environment-the modern and the primitive, the plush and the pristine. Friction is present in every great room.

Combine the ornately traditional with the simplicity of a modern piece. Take the softness of wood and position it right next to the luster of metals. The shiny with the flat, the smooth with the textured, the rustic with the polished glass. This is friction at its best.

It provides the rhythm, that unexpected something that creates a harmonious whole. This is the secret, the hidden surprise in a truly delightful room.

■ *Metal is a mineral that is often overlooked and treated as a stepchild in the extended family of precious metals. The use of metal in this elegant bathroom interior is inspired, and when one adds the finishing touches of white lilies and lit candles; the final effect is almost magical.*

■ *The sheer permanence of materials like stone and metal can evoke a sense of purpose in a room like this kitchen, which gleams with the shine of metal and glows with the luster of polished granite.*

erhaps that's the reason we love our rocks and gems so much. Maybe that's why we feel so pleased when we surround ourselves with them. Because rocks and stones, gems and minerals are like nothing else on earth. And somewhere in our souls, their distinctive brilliance makes us feel right at home.

"If you want a golden rule that will fit everybody, this is it: Have nothing in your houses that you do not know to be useful, or believe to be beautiful."

■ *William Morris*

Seeing the effect of stone next to wood is to be reminded that this tableau often occurs in nature. The final touches of wildflowers and polished rocks, along with the red clay color of the stone wash basin, leads one to imagine that this interior space could almost be an exterior space.

W‌e use them to immortalize ourselves. From the Pyramids at Giza to the Roman Coliseum, the Arc de Triomphe to Mount Rushmore, human greatness is commemorated through the use of stone.

Our admiration of their permanence is evident in common phrases. To convey sturdiness and reliability, we refer to things, and even people, as being "like a rock." Unchangeable items are said to be "set in stone."

■ *The metallic faces of these kitchen cabinets give a fresh, updated look to this kitchen. There is a blending of the old and the new in this space. The silver from the cabinets is repeated again in the legs of the table in the adjoining room. This is a clear demonstration that silver is a strong design element when used in the correct way.*

The babble of a cool mountain stream, the whisper of mist on your upturned face, the exuberance of ocean waves—water quenches a thirst that is physical and spiritual. Glass can create the same flow and buoyancy that is the essence of water. Here, a contemporary etched glass panel at the entrance to the Great Room delights the senses with its graceful presence.

Let the Water Fall

Nothing stills the soul like the sound of water. The roar of waves crashing against a coastline. The babble of a stream rushing busily through a field. The whisper of rain on pavement. The steady trickle of a fountain, splashing on polished stones.

Water quenches a thirst that is both physical and spiritual. It soothes, it caresses, it washes us clean. No matter where you are-dipping your hands in a glacial spring or rolling up the cuffs of your jeans to wade knee-deep into a lake-you can feel the exhilaration that water brings with it.

Water World

It affects all the senses, overwhelming us with beauty on all sides. Your nose twitches in the sea-salt air, air so heavy with the ocean that you can taste it. Your eyes search for the line where the water melts into the sky. Your feet dance in and out of the waves while the surf pounds a rhythm into your head. You are thoroughly drawn in, entranced, invigorated.

Floating on your back in the midst of it, you can feel your knotted muscles begin to relax. It's as close as we can get to flying, weightless, through the blue of the sky with our heads in the clouds.

In all its forms, water bewitches us. Layers of fog, inches of ice, rivers of rain-it's all enchanting. And we want to be as close to it as we can at all times.

"Dreams pass into the reality of action. From the action stems the dream again; and this interdependence produces the highest form of living..."

■ *Anaïs Nin*

We already have it in our homes in the most basic of forms to drink and to wash with. But as a purely decorative, sensory element, it's easy to leave it out. Fortunately, it's just as easy to bring it back.

The Other Water

You can bring the restorative properties of water into your personal space with an aquarium or a small fountain. Or you can use glass to mimic the feeling of water.

Some may think that the use of glass in the creation of a room, such as a glass countertop in a bathroom, marks that room with a "contemporary" style. But it doesn't have to be so. Glass can work in any environment-from the traditional to the modern-because its main purpose is to create the feeling of buoyancy in a room.

Just as water reflects and moves in a continuous stream, glass is a texture that flows and shines. Glass can create a liquid feeling of buoyancy within a room. From the shining, glass-topped counter and gleaming, multi-paned windows to the reflective, mirrored panels at the end of the over-sized bath, this bathroom evokes the shimmer and shine that is the essence of water.

Glass produces flow in a room. Just as water flows in a continuous liquid stream, glass is a texture that flows. Even as a solid material, it carries the same grace as water, the same luminous sensation of softness. For instance, our minds know that a glass counter is a dense, heavy object. But our senses perceive it as soft and light.

When we bend over a body of water, it mirrors our world back to us. And when the sun casts its beams on a liquid surface, you see the thousands of diamond tips sparkling back in reply.

In a day and age where we take everything so seriously, water restores us. It soothes, it caresses, it washes us clean. Here, the graceful bowl that seems to float on the luminous blue glass, the serenity of the swan-like curves of the water fixtures and even the ripples of the gently flickering candles work in water-like harmony to still the soul.

Glass has the same ability. It casts a reflection, it mirrors light. Most of all, it creates a contrast of texture that is infinitely interesting to us, both to our eyes and to our sense of touch. It is with the attention to this kind of intimate detail that the craft of interior design can really make a difference.

The Details Make the Difference

There is an old adage that says, "God is in the details." I firmly believe this to be true in interior design. The details are what really matter, in the end. If you leave out the fine points like texture and creating a sense of flow, you leave out the pieces that enrich a room, that make it a nurturing environment. You cannot ignore the details and still create a room that feels good.

Our eyes may often skip over these little things, but our hearts always take them in. You don't have to be a designer at all to just intuitively know that a room is wonderfully put together because it just feels right.

One of the best reasons to use glass in design is the simple fact of what it does to us. This is a day and age when we all take ourselves and everything we do so seriously. When we are living with materials like glass and water, materials that create a soothing flow and an impression of lightness in our environment, we can loosen up a little.

Environments like these help us to shake off that heavy seriousness and just enjoy the little things that make life worth living. For an interior designer, there is no higher calling.

The fragrance of dew dappled roses, the taste of a tomato fresh from the vine, the warming orange color of pumpkins in the fall—flowers and vegetables please all our senses. This dining room is enhanced by the flowers on the table and the picture of a pepper on the wall. Complementing the wood of the table and in the cabinetry, these flowers and fruits also bring with them a sense of freshness and vitality.

As the Garden Grows...

Sometimes they take you by surprise. You walk past a pile of green and think,"Was that...?" and you bend over for a look, and sure enough. A gorgeous yellow bell pepper smiles at you from beneath the leaves. Or maybe it was the shy purple violet, nestled in the spring grass beside the sidewalk.

Flowers, fruits and vegetables work a special kind of magic. They seem simple in nature, but are often complicated in their loveliness—so many intricate stems and petals, so many indescribable variations of color. They throw their beauty at you in the garden, in the forest, in city gardens and on country lanes. And there's always enough variety to have something for everyone.

The kitchen can be a garden of nature's bounty as well as a place to eat. Here, the fruit design on the seat cushions, the valance and on the inset tiles is enhanced by the vibrant colors of the living plants and flowers. This "garden atmosphere" provides a natural and warm counterpoint to the often impersonal looking appliances you find in a kitchen.

Veggie and Fruit Tales

Vegetables and fruits have such wholesome beauty. They hold a nourishing promise of health and ripe, juicy mouthfuls of goodness. And they have a way of making us happy just because we're around them.

The apple orchards, showering you with blossoms in the spring and then popping out all over in delicious reds and yellows that beg to be picked. The twisting vines of fat red tomatoes. The perfect Halloween pumpkin. The taste of sweet corn roasted on a campfire.

Sometimes they evoke a powerful memory of a specific time or place. That amazing pineapple you had for breakfast on your honeymoon in Puerto Vallarta. All those perfect little sugar peas you shelled with your grandmother on the front steps of her farmhouse.

Flowers by the Dozen

Flowers make us feel just as deeply. Can you remember what flowers lined the aisles at your wedding? Or what that first Prom corsage smelled like? How about the time you discovered that the yellow stuff on dandelions could rub off on someone's face and leave a bright yellow stain?

There always seems to be a flower for all seasons, no matter where you are. Christmas Poinsettias. Easter Lilies. Fall Chrysanthemums. Summer Bougainvillaea.

Flowers, by their very nature, signify emotions. Happy yellows. Flirtatious pinks. Somber russets. We pick them—and buy them—for every occasion. Weddings, births, deaths, birthdays, anniversaries and all those "Just because-es" and "I'm sorries."

Flowers give us a whole new language with which we can express in color and texture and form, all the things we cannot find the words to say. No wonder we want to bring them all inside.

So we bring them in—the almost ripe tomatoes and the perky spring tulips. We pick them on the roadside or in our own gardens or buy them from a hothouse. We arrange them with so much care, in exquisite vases and homey bowls. We want to bring the living things inside, we want them to bring that spark of life to our rooms. And so they do.

It has been said that living flowers are an example of the eternal seductiveness of life, and here in this elegant kitchen, they provide the spark that gives the area focus. The tones of fuschia, orange, yellow, green and purple beautifully set off the black granite tabletop and accessories and provide a colorful and vivacious accent to this sophisticated kitchen.

■ *This sunny room is alive with color—from the bright yellow sunflowers to the burnished red walls and the woven floor rug. The final effect is one that lifts your spirits and reminds you of the beauty that can be found in plants, flowers and the world in general.*

A Garden Inside

Once indoors, it's usually the color that arrests the senses first. The glistening white of a delicate orchid. The exuberant green of a fresh lime. It's amazing what those spots of other-worldly color can do to a room. Sometimes boldly, sometimes quietly, they assume center stage. You can't help but stare in their direction.

They make a room feel cared for. You see a bouquet of flowers, and you wonder how it got there. Surely someone gave it as a token of love; someone took the time to pick and choose the best shapes and colors to convey just the right emotion.

And then there is the fragrance that comes with them. The hint of a rainy day clinging to the leaves of a freshly picked daisy. The fragrance of moist earth, warming in the sun, that rises from the cheeks of a ripening tomato. The aroma of Florida orange groves and California vineyards, the humid green of Midwest cornfields and the salt spray of the eastern seaboard.

Living things brought indoors carry in such a vibrant, glowing feeling of life. Our minds recognize and react to that on some unconscious level. It's as if everywhere we go, our minds are searching for some relief from sameness. We crave something unique, something different, something alive. What can be more unique than the simple beauty of these living things?

The Rule of Thumb

And the best part about creating a garden inside is that every petal, every fruit, every last shape and shade of vegetable always matches everything else that's going on! Some people try to carefully plan which shade of pink will best complement their rose colored room. But they don't have to.

As in nature outdoors, so in our homes—the color of flowers and vegetables goes with anything. Red flowers can go in a blue room, an orange room, a pink room...it doesn't matter. Every flower in every size matches everything you have.

It's one of my favorite things about designing interiors—looking to nature and following its lead. Because in great design, good design and ordinary design, there is only one cardinal rule. And that rule is—there are no rules!

A Day at the Beach

Doesn't everyone have one perfect day at the beach at least once in a lifetime? A day when the sun smiled down, turning the sand into a glittering field of gold. A day that was not too hot and not at all cold. When the sand warmed your bare feet and the sun warmed your bare head. You plopped down on a blanket, slid on your sunglasses, cracked open that juicy novel and sat back to spend an entire day doing nothing important at all.

Maybe that day hasn't happened yet, but every time you find yourself sinking your toes into a pile of sand, you hope that it is on its way.

A summer day with sun and sand can relax every muscle in your body and make you want to stretch out like a cat. An elegant sunroom can engender the same feeling by evoking the warmth of a summer day. The sunny hue of these wood furnishings, the vibrant green of the living plant and the light through the window create a feeling of warmth and peace that is the essence of sun and sand. Even at night, this room can put you in a sunny mood.

Summer Daze

It just does something to us, the combination of sun and sand. It rests us and warms us and fills us with light. It promises time to relax with friends, with lovers, with children and with dogs who catch Frisbees. Time to build sandcastles and search for strange looking shells and salt-encrusted driftwood.

"Come forth into the light of things,
Let Nature be your teacher."
■ *William Wordsworth*

It brings back the feeling of how summer used to be at the beginning of June, when school was out and the months stretched before you in long, lazy afternoons of furious bike riding and quickly melting ice cream cones.

It makes you feel the way a cat does when it finds a spot of sun to stretch out and yawn in, and then curl around itself to take a good nap.

But unless you're one of the few lucky souls whose backyard is a beach, spending a day in sand and sun usually means either a long trip in the car or a square sandbox at the playground. So maybe you never thought you could bring that sandy, sunny feeling home with you. But you can.

■ *Fabrics inspired by the colors of sun and sand can automatically brighten your spirits. The hand-dyed fabrics used on this daybed beautifully illustrate this point. The tawny gold on the cushion and the sun design that graces the pillows make this welcoming spot the perfect place for daytime dreams of childhood summers building sandcastles on the beach.*

■ *The careful use of accessories and a warm, golden palette of color invite the relaxing power of sun and sand into this windowless powder room. The rich color of the woodwork and cabinetry, the stylized sunrays surrounding the mirror and even the soap and living flowers seem to infuse this small room with glowing light.*

Let the Sun Shine In

You can bring the sun and sand inside in so many small ways, with texture and color and certain shades of yellow. You can use the golden hue of soft woods to recreate the tawny sense of sand. You can choose cozy furniture like those big sofas that just pull you in, as snug as the biggest beach blanket.

But above all else, you can let the sun shine in any way you want.

A room like this doesn't have heavy draperies or darkened windows. It's not a serious place built with serious materials. It is a soft place. It has skylights and big windowpanes, open doors and open spaces.

"Happiness comes of the capacity to feel deeply, to enjoy simply, to think freely, to risk life and be needed."
■ *Storm Jamison*

And believe it or not, a room like this doesn't depend on 365 bright sunny days a year to successfully create its cheery attitude.

The colors of sun and sand can create a feeling of peace and softness in even the most elegant room. This Great Room radiates with a gentle light from windows open to the sky and glows with the light tones of yellow that are found on the walls and in the furnishings. Even on a cold winter day, it suggests the warmth of a summer day.

■ *This welcoming kitchen provides the feeling of warmth that a day of sand and sun can invoke. As a favorite family gathering place, there's no better spot to fill with the colors of the beach. From the window that reflects the sun's relaxing rays to the sand-hued cabinetry and golden counter lighting, this room makes everyone feel warm, relaxed and filled with light.*

A Sunny Disposition

A room that speaks of sand and sun isn't limited to being a daytime room, because the spirit of sunlight exists independent of the hour or the weather. That's why this sort of room feels sunny even on the dreariest, cloudiest day.

Its personality is inherent in the tiny little details of texture, color and space.

Rooms like this offer a standing invitation that says, "Walk right in here and sit yourself down." These are rooms that are not background rooms. They are not intimidating rooms, either. They just make you feel the way a beach feels—warm and serene and full of light. And best of all, they reflect that sense of light back onto the people who occupy the rooms.

This room is designed to make you feel as warm and cozy as your toes feel when you sink them into a mound of soft, warm sand. Here, the warm, tawny color of sand predominates, and, when combined with soft, cushy furniture, embraces you with comfort, creating a feeling of relaxation reminiscent of sun and sand.

Rooms inspired by sand and sun automatically brighten your spirits, to the point that if you were in a really bad mood, being in a room like this would either change your frame of mind or you would have to find some dark corner to skulk in. Somehow, in creating a room like this, you harness that effervescent quality that all human beings have within them, and you turn it into a very physical, tangible quality.

Clients who love rooms like this are people who just want things to be beautiful. They may not actually say how much they love the beach. They may have never even been to a beach. But they love to be near the glow of the sun.

I think everyone needs a happy sun room at some point in their lives. Because there is no power on earth like that of sunshine—the power to warm you to your very core.

Dark chocolate, cocoa, mocha—the many tones of brown one can find in nature are rich in their beauty, diverse in their numbers and have the ability to be as sophisticated or casual as you choose. On this elegant antique piece, the deep, dark brown and gleaming gold found in nature lends an air of sophistication. When enhanced by the light brown in the picture frame, the dark chocolate of the lampshade and the sparkle of the silver tea service, this area exhibits a rich personality all its own.

Mocha, Cocoa & Chocolate
(From Nature to Nurture)

Chocolate is actually a pretty emotional subject. It is not like other candies. It has the distinction of being one of the most favorite treats ever. There is something about this delicacy, in all its forms, that warms the heart like nothing else.

■ Bringing the flavor of chocolate into your home can help you unwind. Here chocolate shows its casual, cozy side as it stars in a room where you can nestle deep into the sofa. The cozy warmth is carried into the kitchen through the use of milk chocolate brown on the chairs.

Chocoholic Tendencies

Think about all the chocolate experiences in your life...

A steaming cup of hot cocoa (with the little marshmallows floating on top) on a cold day. The thick, gooey icing on your birthday cake. Fresh fudge, stocked with chunks of walnut. The Valentine boxes full of mystery chocolates—the ones you have to bite into to find out what's inside. The simple joy of a Hershey's bar®, (both with and without almonds). That huge solid chocolate Easter bunny that dares you to devour it all in one sitting.

Brownies. Mocha. Pudding. Milkshakes.

This same appetite for chocolate that is making your stomach rumble and your mouth water can also make you feel at home.

"Giving chocolate to others is an intimate form of communication, a sharing of deep, dark secrets."

■ *Milton Zelman*

The smooth, velvety comfort you get from biting into a delicious piece of imported chocolate is the experience you receive as you sink into this cozy and relaxing living room. Toffee tones drawn in from the walls, coffee table and pillow accents blended with the cocoa colors of the sofa and chairs cue in a delicious flavor into this delightful room. The welcoming feel this space gives makes it perfect for entertaining friends.

Homemade Chocolate

Does it come as a surprise, then, that bringing the flavor of chocolate into your home can help you relax and unwind? The feeling of chocolate can be achieved in so many ways, with so many shades of brown.

Creating a chocolate room is, simply, setting a specific mood. It's not about contrast or foreground or playful or serious. It's just about the general feeling a room provides. Rooms can use brown without being a chocolate room. Because a room that says "chocolate" is a room where you want to nestle deep into the sofa and stay there for a really, really long time. It's a warm and solid room that is somehow sophisticated at the same time. It's vibrant, not frumpy.

And though the room is balanced, there is no specific focal point, because you don't need one in a room like this. This is the kind of room where you just need to "be."

■ *With the desk set perfectly into the space, who could help but spend the afternoon using their imagination writing letters and poems. Set in the soothing tone of browns, you're sure to have peaceful nap, or simply just daydream--of chunky mountains of chocolate and lakes of mocha, of course!*

■ Use your imagination to smell the flavors of this room: toffee lacing a vanilla wafer, as found in the carpet trim; a playful mix of white chocolate and almonds displayed in the fabric of the chairs. Take another minute to smell the aroma of cocoa arising from the table and chairs. The rich flavor of mocha abounds from the beautifully displayed cabinet.

■ *Flavorful mocha, cocoa and chocolate fills the room in color and breath as you enter this richly styled room. The smooth darkness of the leather--like large chunks of dark chocolate; the shiny, almost ebony piano--as if gazing into a hot cup of rich mocha. This is lovely space for music, coffee, and friends.*

The Most Comfortable Room in the House

I created a chocolate room in my own home, a nice warm room with brown walls and a stone fireplace, just off my kitchen. The couch is easy to lose yourself in. The carpet is comfortable. It's a book-reading room. A staring-into-the fire room. A sit on the floor and talk with your friends until 2 a.m. kind of room.

"There's nothing better than a good friend,
except a good friend with chocolate."

■ *Linda Grayson, in The Pickwick Papers*

There is an ease about it. It contains nothing questionable or difficult. It's as if the room itself loses focus when you are in it. It makes you feel like, well... like you're enjoying some truly excellent chocolate.

The beauty of imagination, as found in this painting, challenges your creativity. It can also be captured in this setting, or any, if you allow it to. The deep, dark hardwood of this elegant chair—like hard chunks of bittersweet dark chocolate. The curves of the chair arms—like the flow of mocha pouring out from the spout of a carafe. In the off white tones of the walls—taste the creamer.

"Hope has a color and it's one children can sense. Here, all the elements of nature I love and cherish combine to transform a facility that helps survivors of sexual abuse into a place of beauty and light."

114

The Color of Hope

We've created nurturing environments where they are most needed. Shelters for the homeless and facilities for women and children of domestic violence are just are just a few of the places where Susan Fredman & Associates has donated expertise and time. We do this because we feel that even furnishings and color can help offer hope and comfort.

We have established a foundation called Supporting the Spirit that will provide pro bono interior design services and donated materials to selected non-profit organizations. This unique design resource gives designers a place to volunteer their time and talents to create more nurturing interior spaces for our non-profit partners.

Healing by Design

It is my hope that after experiencing this book, you will see your world with new eyes. You'll see the spirit of the trees in an oak table, hear the rush of water in a glass wall. You'll remember how the sky makes you feel at peace as you paint your bedroom wall just the right shade of blue.

Your world is transformed once you've uncovered the beauty of nature and made it your own.

So where do you go from here? Once you put this book down, what projects will you pick up? And if you truly believe, as I do, that design makes a difference, how then will you wield that difference?

One of the ongoing projects that has given me the most joy in the past 25 years happened almost without my thinking about it. But once I paused to consider it, I saw that it made perfect sense. It was the perfect way to use my design skills to make a difference.

In Need of Healing

In the course of my career, as my desire to design nurturing interiors has grown, I have noticed something that bothers me.

Research has proven how much our environments influence and affect our behavior patterns, our sense of well being, our ability to work productively, and even our capacity to heal. But the places that are most in need of a nurturing environment, the places whose very purpose is to create well-being and to help us heal—these are the places where the environment is often most neglected.

"Millions of men have lived to fight, build palaces and boundaries, shape destinies and societies; but the compelling force of all times has been the force of originality and creation profoundly affecting the roots of human spirit."

■ *Ansel Adams*

Shelters for the homeless and battered women and children, hospices, childcare facilities... these are the places where people strive so diligently to mend broken spirits and offer comfort and hope. And yet because many of these non-profit organizations operate on very limited budgets, they can't afford to consider whether the wall color in their reception room casts a comforting glow. They just have to make do with what they have. And too many times, the outcome is dismal.

The people who work to provide care in these organizations are not nurtured by their surroundings. And the people who come there for help often can't wait to leave—not because of the services or programs offered, but because the physical space just makes them feel unsettled and uncomfortable.

The space, in essence, is the program. You can't have an effective program if your environment is working against you.

The Color of Hope

For nearly 25 years now, we at Susan Fredman & Associates have thrown ourselves into this cause—to create nurturing environments where they are most needed. In places like LaCASA, the Lake County Council Against Sexual Assault, we designed every detail of their 13,000 square-foot space. We've provided services for Orchard Village, a home for developmentally disabled people, and for shelters like Deborah's Place.

We've found that there are so many leftover materials which, when recycled, can transform a shelter or childcare center into a place of beauty and light. So wherever we can, we use donated and recycled materials to re-energize a place, and by doing so we encourage the staff who works there and replenish the spirits of those who come for help.

It's amazing how well it works! When the environment supports the cause, a non-profit agency has more opportunity to nurture its community, to become more productive, and to enhance the quality of care it delivers. It becomes a place of hope and comfort that lives and breathes, not only in its mission statement, but in every inch of its being, from floor to ceiling.

The mission and the environment become inseparable. They both hold out the tangible promise and color of hope.

Supporting the Spirit

As we move into the future of our company, this ongoing mission of enhancing the environments of non-profit organizations has become something that is very important for Susan Fredman & Associates. So we've decided to make it official.

We are establishing a foundation that will provide pro bono interior design services and donated materials to selected non-profit organizations, thereby making us a design resource for our non-profit community. And we are calling this foundation Supporting the Spirit.

It just makes sense. Supporting the Spirit Foundation offers designers a place to go to volunteer their time and talents; it serves as a clearinghouse for furniture and materials that cannot be sold, and it offers non-profit organizations a resource that they may never have had access to.

As we embark on this venture, we have several goals in mind. We want to raise awareness and educate others about this important connection between proper design and the well-being of staff and clients. We want to provide a combination of design services, materials, furniture and fixtures to fulfill the needs of our non-profit partners, and we want to create an inventory of donated and recycled goods.

We want to develop a team of interior designers who will form the basis of the foundation's work. The more design professionals who come together through Supporting the Spirit, the more organizations will be served.

Personally, I can't imagine a better way for designers to put their skills to work. Imagine the difference we can make...

We can bring the sky to earth. We can surround children who are ill with the twitter of birds and the bright faces of flowers. We can comfort the frightened with the solidity of forest trees and bring the warmth of sunshine to those who are without hope. With our design, we can support their spirits.

To learn more about Supporting the Spirit Foundation, call (847) 509-4121, ext. 41.

SUPPORTING THE SPIRIT FOUNDATION
The Design Resource
for the Nonprofit Community

Acknowledgments

It is most important to acknowledge the people who make our work possible. Our vendors provide the product, but that is just a bare minimum of what they do. We count on them to deliver the best quality product available, to deliver it on time (please) and at a fair price. We know that our relationship is precious and that it is circular, as well, because neither one of us can survive without the other. In the same way, we know that our vendors have the utmost regard and respect for the clients that we share. And because of this, we have a priceless partnership.

We profusely thank the following vendors for their generous support.

Deerpath Carpet
838 N. Western Avenue
Lake Forest, Illinois 60045

Abitare Inc.
1301 Merchandise Mart
Chicago, Illinois 60654

Marble Emporium
613 W. 16th Street
Chicago, Illinois, 60616

Cabinet & Counter
1750 W. Fulton Street
Chicago, Illinois 60612

Benchmark Cabinetry
Rambo Cabinetry
KitchenCraft Cabinetry
c/o Lamico Designers
20614 Milwaukee Avenue
Deerfield, Illinois 60015

deitelbloom rugs intl. inc
1655 Merchandise Mart
Chicago, Illinois 60654

Designs Alive, Ltd.
1061 High Street
Mundelein, Illinois 60060

Equally as important are the architects, builders and general contractors who share our dream of creating a truly sensational home, with all the special little details such a place can provide. We enjoy working with you. We count on you. And we know that all of our work is manifested at its very best because of your teamwork with us.

And most importantly, I would like to thank the people of Susan Fredman & Associates, Ltd. Our staff has grown through the years to almost 25 members. We work every day as a team, seeking to collaborate and co-create. And we do well to honor the differences and distinctions that each of us bring to the table.

Thank You to...

Lonnie Unger, who brings almost 15 years of energy and dedication to her position as Executive Vice President.

Susan Rossie, our COO, who is dedicated to seeing our company grow and flourish.

Tracey Duffy, the all-seeing, all-knowing eyes for everyone at SFA. She keeps us all on track.

Gail Costa and Janet Thurber, who make sure that we are financially sound. Their dedication keeps everyone and everything running smoothly.

Our amazing team of extremely talented designers: Judy Gordon, Lani Myron, Rosemary Ryan, Carrie Engelhaupt, Missie Cohen, Linda Eisenberg, Cheryl Kling, Jody Gruel, Carly Sax, Ruth Mortensen, Martha Teten and Sheila Gutrich. Their creativity and insight make great interior design work look so easy.

To the staff of SFA, thank you so for allowing me the privilege of knowing and working with each and every one of you. I have grown as a person and as a professional because of the difference that each of you make.